ABSENCE LIKE SUN

VINCENT A. CELLUCCI

Absence Like Sun
Vincent A. Cellucci

Printed in the U.S.A.
First Printing
10 9 8 7 6 5 4 3 2 1   18 19 20 21 22 23

Book design by the author
Cover Art: Christina Johnson, "Breach 5" (2012)
Internal Art: Sean Goebel, "Digital Petroglyphs" (2018)

Library of Congress Control Number: 2018965159
Cellucci, Vincent A.
Absence Like Sun / Vincent A. Cellucci;
p. cm.
ISBN: 978-1-944884-60-4 (pbk.)

Lavender Ink
lavenderink.org

acknowledgements

absolute thanks and appreciation to the publishers and editors of the following publications, where previous manifestations of these poems appeared:

"a nother / anaphora" *Horse Less Review #17

"applause of the dead" *Deluge

"crash   the sun emerges" *Tender_loin

"deported oarsmen" and
    "send someone close   second to none" *Unlikely Stories

"diamonds in dystopia" *Best American Experimental Writing 2018

"infanticide sunsets," "from above the andes," and
    "america" *Truck

"jaws of life" *Xavier Review 37.2

"nothing / nothing to the very last drop" and
    "french me in the dungeon" *VIATORdc

"park poem" *The Berkeley Poetry Review #44

"self portrait" *moria vol 13 issue 2

"suns stacked russian" *so and so mag #7

"volcano belly" *Fuck Poems an exceptional anthology

"where the wind becomes water" *Dusie #17
    (In Memoriam Marthe Reed)

"your sun's what they come for / when they come for you" *Topology

table of contents

to my family
for your enduring support

and especially to Kimberly
my guiding sister in absence

I will still be making poems for you
Out of silence;
Silence will be falling into that silence,
It is building music

—Muriel Rukeyser

Joy against nothingness
By the wrack we shall sing our Sun-song

—Louis Zukofsky

I am the son of death

my first word was light

your sun's what they come for
when they come for you

i.

I silence sun
only in the desert
seams increase the difference
degrees between night and day

horizons shrivel
squinting oasis
our symbols sand

mercy saturates
stars
still the expanse

ii.

I have no flock pride or pack

even the sun has constellations
the river tributaries

is there such a thing as a tree or forest
us versus the masses

these night questions hatch
til dawn gathers light and gloom

my absence knows no borders

Arise,

darling   give me your young

& silent words

remove platters of impossible

off the planet

hostage moribund

fortune lacking sequel

opening coda

abundant earth replicas
reply *I no longer speak wind*
you're misplaced too
divided by the Father
and last night I had that baby
rattlesnake dancing dream
the one when you can't step
away each strike a missed bite
infant venom glands spray
slithering death confined me to toll around
collapse skyways beneath the scaled trees
delve into hell on top of a cloud

Sometime joys   fill eldests

unapologetic nothingness

from shores emerge mtns

may rumble again

defend us from the power

of earth

conceived from dead worlds

a lagoon shoreless

kisses surface

soaked skin peels

infanticide sunsets

To Robert Creeley

spindle over the shoulder tossing gills
pulse to pleasure
covered knees locked
gusher under sea   father flattens family
one must be a sniper & assassinate the adult
committing infanticide in us all
don't ask offerings   ask sandboxes
empty swing sets   slides
or the rivers full of kittens
the mirrors who've seen enough faces
as the seer darkness
the sword stomachs
the sea tempests
or horizons gold thieves
            gimmie a break baby
                        & i'll return the century

a child raised right taking back my first stolen piece of candy

park poem

in the city women elderly east
either eat biscuit snacks or throw down cards
chips and cash cavort around a stone table
in columbus park
only other whites admire a rat
shares my bench with a cane in a corner away
from the more serious games
interrupted by intermittent blows from a fella on sax
taps his sneakered beat and someone joins on flute now
two strings no harmony only humanity passing
the day on benches in between buildings two snake-skin
banjos begin to organize the sound into the first time
I haven't thought about love's failures or death today I can
relish the poem smoke from a gentleman's pipe
the drunk's disheveled hair   fruit fingers   admiring eyes
we all wander
bye our unsettled song
fills and drains meager moments plucking
misery and amusement until it gets too cold
in the park it's time to leave
go home
if we don't have one
make one

Absent are those who are

cast out shadows each night

and die   long before we save

violence collects light blinding

beyond the visible

in the offing   of words

in direct opposition

to the inevitable

worn in

this world

granulates us

where the wind becomes water

For Zack Godshall

we spent the morning like drug money
clutching our guts in rest stops
sped past listened limits crossed
the crucifixion of the lost and old
river   city shadows
       lost losin
       depression

escapee sights resume
                  paved sprawl of the american soul
                  big rig squall
     safety's a battering ram
          crimes against natural
        sound of a child's ass hitting playground slide
         fall of
market forest rv aborigine
shaking tugboat every turn
       marry the barge yard to
           the cudd company
       spaghetti highways to skyline
          the rio to san jacinto
         we used to be kin
         now we quarrel
               race
            to drown the barrel
                 of emptied grass seed
                 drawing **88** cents a lb.

    surely there are other ways
    to dispose of these bargains
              & blessings
           gambled away
—hid here—

    in the shriveled skin of a desert dweller
    or the decomposing hairs cacti sunder

        we climbed past
        the helve rock altar
        to where the wind becomes water

many of us

For Chris Tonelli

measure
our life in second chances
the storms didn't worship
away forgiven faults our family
fondly recalls
a rotten pier
extending into the polluted sea

many of us
are composed of warring countries
we seldom extend ourselves treatises
too often horizon we habituate
the horror infinite
as granite

many of us
seldom fortunate
in our assembled armament
but buoyant in beliefs of lasting
commiserate the malefic commandment

squint into sky
the clouds past casting
dark continents on the backdrop of sea
hunkered away from heaven

Sorrow smiles

blessed be the neglected

for theirs

we divide

separating remains

ransom

if day kept
    all arguments
        the fuckin
        the *what's-his-fuckin-names*

unsatisfied bags of groceries
bestowed from the search
of fluttered lives

    how serpentine combines
        keeps finders   little places

to give or take   from the weak

    under canopy's rain
    a solar yearling
        like when I got my first body
  I roamed romantic   *chirped at boys*   *contorted*
        with bella donnas
        our pranks digested
        in galleries

exhibit the last rays of light
spectacle solid as the shelter
  of silence begging for a breath

    irrefutable life
        what some might now even consider:
    it or I
      the cleaver

abundance of one

panther's skin spread over the snow beneath the stars

—text from Joseph Cornell's
Taglioni's Jewel Casket

ask the air how it breathes
a square where it gets cornered
is there an abundance in one?

we each have an abundance
there are so many of me
I can't choose
no centrifuge
can separate
the selves which switch
scales keeping pace
with meteor showers how
we fall in and out

soul   lessons   lie
like Polaris in constancy
an axis implies one
but one needs three to exist

our society syzygy
instead of being
we went from
colony to urban
users online

while some muster
cyber militia
my mutiny blinks
at memory's fission
and we diffuse alien
to monitor mirrors
replace the mob and
all the elements we deplete
one by one from abundance

mine the universe
when we get there
one day all of us will leave
this planet exodus invasive
departing for one habitable
territory determined by its abundance

open some time

we lather
          looseness   corks on the steps
                                            cities   moles
                                              on coarse earth hide

      envision invasion
          & time on its turquoise
          pushcarts of ciao
          wobbles forward
                    jump star

we worst in our knows
          future
          is our foe
                cups mouth with the fingers of his favored hand
                    so no one can see what was spoken here

The last word

uttered by the most magnificent

                                     ventriloquist

holds you

hiding in plain sight

Absence *I am*   *here*

shining

down

look into the people light attracts

the last resort   my first step

shhh darling we leave   on repeat

soon cease

sun common

a spine   across   the sea

          exhales dawn on my arm

          breaks cloud wakes

      hiding heavens'
      placidity abandoned here when

sun evolved
    to soot
      books you have machines to read
         drones to rove

         all hours
           their hours

army of earth liberated combustion   the globe smothered internal
    our callouses refused
       debts acquiesced
         this blaring silence

jets us   hands to dreams
       fusion pursed
       pets our hides

   river lassos my larynx
   constricts blood
   tugs these buoys
       bobbing in the tide
       we must not survive

nothing
nothing to the very last drop

To Salgado Maranhão, Santiago Vizcaíno, and Alexis Levitin

the horizon shoulders
    crucified youth
on ceiba spikes
one shucked eye

wise to the will
of the altitude
   and colorful coup
wedding crisscrossing
window clothesline
empty pins hold

a bus   most won't exit
or get on

& always the breeze
enlists the day
bribing the limbs of bushes
for a blessing

defeated by
motor commotion

plastic bags
suffocate the wind

not important
   not impossible

   it just hasn't rained
for the first day in days

Unguent universe

replace our origin   converse

blow out the centerpiece

emits

beyond the zenith

how many hold habitable

hone a second

abode

manhattan anyone in earshot

on crutches
this crucial life
     hobbles past tables
        two cellulars apiece
        posthumans tap

I have a hunk of triple cream melting
            in my bag
            & my baguette
                    spears the busboy
                    running tubs
I apologize
        check out the waitress
 repent my apology
    keep writing
      imbibing
          secret sentiments
                bestow curses
                passenger masses
                delayed
                    subway sick
                        sound of a barstool
                      as it scoots back
            we all frame
                the streets   gallery

summon someone
        with a crowbar
        slim jim
        or celebrity
           common as cellophane
           cheap linen aprons
                tossed piled stained
        just out of
          sight   black hole
                      of side towels

banned from
the filial brasserie
lights dimmer grow

        we forbid what's been foretold
        bemoan what's been bestowed

humbling hangover

it's snowing   I can't eat
                    I'm napping
  in the harold washington library

there is a conference filling the hilton
but today I can't bear them
nor can I afford a room

              public makes more sense to me

I rode the escalators
saw sight lines from the top floor
& overheard the vietnam vets
swap mud clogging their barrels stories—

I rest with the homeless lady next to me
sorting her bags within bags
wombs for lugging her every nothing
belonging   she finishes
                  examines her worn soles

I am lucky to have so many lessons
      packed and laid out before me

      she must feel secure
      she left her things
while she went away—

I'll watch them

america

I'm the styrofoam
                    sleepyhead to seduce you

            icicle fangs
            melt for sunrise
    between thighs   slowpoke round back
    morning attack
                    sheathed erect
                    crowned copper
go extravagant
                delinquents

                        my sister's
                        a slap
                        & the hardest kick
                        to the balls I know

the secret of no love
                    divulged

        judged by behavior
        bye bye love
        bye bye savior

                    lions kneel
                    gazelles govern
        & silent words sacrifice poems
let you down   have idiosyncrasies   dents
                    favorite colors
                        and foods
why not the rum cake our parents served
                at their divorce
                now I taste
                young
                    survivors
                        tucked like words in wills

the howling outside my door
                does not disturb me

freedom makes the best slaves

Liberty's widow

concussed cuckold

all   owns   thee

useless competing on behalf

of anything that ends

dying discount

free for all

selling a world

that lasts

suns stacked russian

                                  apart
our menace is mismanaged
my sincerity is severity
can't go where the river ends
friends bury friends bury lovers
strangers terrorize each other
         beveled we encapsulate
our menace is severe
our sincerity is mismanaged
zero zenith shine
                inseparable—

Tonight behave as death's child

awake staring into the pupils of

here

preserved prayers become an emptiness

around which our dreams churn & sputter

evaporated

hole only a stranger
                    can fill
            when we reach
        charged moments
        dim bulbs grow grapefruit
suspended from the cupids at st. joe's
        someone's struggling everyone
            equal to the patrons warming their hands
                        & faces over
                        iphones
        my poor dehorned
        body a stethoscope
        cold shock spans ceiling
            beams resin
                incense heat rising
                wash   rinse   enlist
    holy stop motion stance dilapidates the animate
            gimbal locking police   handle all talking
            nemesis got our patio closed
            & my wrist is rocking restoration
                all bottled up nonentity
                waiting to walk
                the trepidation
                    trapeze
                    pulled up
                    gratuitous as
                    gravity

sun and drang

in the east
a man   every morning
collects his family
will not work
until he commands
the sun to rise
but he's wise
enough not to
demand   until it
of its own accord
appears on the horizon

it is his nature
to revere
again he says: *certainly!*

this wretched soil
has been tilled
a thousand years

activity continues
eternity to eternity
seems to set
only on our earthly eyes
in reality
never sets
but shines
on unceasingly

we should only utter
higher maxims
so far as they can benefit
the world   the rest
we should keep

within they will diffuse
over our actions a luster
like the mild radiance
of a gathering storm

Relentless bleeding

horizons restore

ancient ceilings

collect

the vapor eternal

I only remember

who is next to me   absence

                          bathing

                                in

so many decrepit

                          words

Sheppardess of the Stars

held fire-threshing bonds

forced matter base

the body passed   out of the body

stripped solstice

love us dying and had to

if I etched
                a tick mark
        every time
                        I wanted to
                    wake you
    I could thatch a roof
      but your slumber cheers for serenity
                        of a continental drift
            your dreams:
                    pangaea
& even if all perpends this placebo
        the roof resides
& no matter how promiscuous it gets
we shall never be homeless in memory

I don't recollect

brief command of company

                idolatry

or the heavens abandoned

how many lovers

have you arranged

to sacrifice paradise

opposed to remembering

Sheppardess of Stars

you are so far sought

stars grow stale

hold a stranger

        fills

      this absence genesis

a nother
anaphora

another of my lovers taught me how to condition my hair
a nother stores glasses right side up in the cabinet
an other turned the toilet paper backwards stressing the ease of pull rather than unroll
a nother let me lick her until I had a vague idea what incredible anatomy really entailed
an other dressed me up   painted toes and braided hair
another picked and popped my skin's imperfections
a nother demanded dinero for the pill morning after
an other treated me too nice so I had to rid myself
another never works out if I don't err
ah the nother that mixed watercolor and black ink letter after letter
       I may still have those although they are stored in the recess
               of corrugated cardboard buried
               beneath boxes in a closet
               that won't have to be packed after they bury me—
another refused me and I'm dead sure where that leaves us
an other's nectar tastes better than her disease
separating a nother from others or another one believes in monogamy
a nother I refuse to share refuses to share me
another played the piano but I pretended to prefer the clarinet
an other plagiarized their content
a nother may often prevent another nother
another always listens cause I never shut the fuck up
a nother silences my thoughts assuaged
avoid an other that gallops self-destructiveness
another pair of eyes to lock or avoid
an other ruptured recognition
another smiles submerged a nother's frowns
another faith impossible all
another time
another galaxy   would be a nother
   an other over body   space
             never
another accident
        that concubine of catastrophe
        another conquistador of selflessness
        pandora's wrapping paper
a nother labors limited
        to link losses
           across lifetimes—

Stroke

of infatuation

unsettled opposite

rises death's ocular

not sure   you have much left

—to learn—

kidnapper bring

my baby back

french me in the dungeon

french me in the dungeon
next to the guy in the headset claiming security
pass the cold drink tongue
tip wants to welcome
lotion the wrong way making me
swallow a sunburn
taste buds slippery and bald
as the greasy styrofoam cup
my palm impaled
to gas lamp ornament   artificial roe
the air   incense
rolls down sewer
thigh highs unruly as river
gust overtures overflow ripe sentiments
spoiling stories of gut rot
abundant exes
and profanity churn
the genius last round
girl I'll make you famous
put your face on a milk carton
won the rejection we all craving
denial season both sides
surges unsuppressed
bonds us in fatal loneliness
when was losing
yourself worthless
how long can you sustain
onlooking tragedy before kicking yourself out

distending solitude

after reading Bolaño's "Lluvia"

To Ben Lowenkron

you can't cry yourself out
into my cama climb

let's claw each other
to avoid the blackness of night

la barca was the name of the bar
braiding its tentacles out front

neon victory defeated tongues
accidently spit a child out

it was the men that made the boy's offense
prey vultures blindfolded by their carrion

leaving the impossible

The moon has a swollen cheek
                                    —Ezra Pound

every swollen war
fingertips salute
            the bella above
            upon cloud throne
                    sunspot traps the top
                                of her thigh
                    where dress has risen
& her hair   the underworld spilling tidal
                                pride replaced
                    captured smitten images

            the moon's contributions   lost oars
            rowing against the celestial swarm

                    chromosphere bound by
                    black lace bra crawls out
                of mother tierra
                granted immaculate skin
            spicules smolder pupils
                            prayers paid
                        our dues   presence
                            stills the
                            twitching

volcano belly

pops out the breakers
as a humpback whale sledgehammers
the ocean into a home
                trying is a: blessing blessing
                    u: the virgin bride
     thrown over cone

    I want pussy praise
like a fucking fire alarm
   in a bank vault
  the corner of a swum soul
  graffitied in
       fuck *singing in the rain*
       fuck writing *poems*
       in the aphotic zone

my hands sign urchins
a tank of squid ink
needling you

   I want your crevice ceviche
             suicide behind

please don't listen to me
I'm going to die

Delinquent decimals   flesh cymbals

clang   caution infinity

distance   silences   our percussion

southerning the bone

For Dylan

we wade in cut years
infested by slithering
loneliness nocturnal pupils
in remote reflections

sky pale drifts cement
crypts hanging moss
submerged sway
of an ancient reptilian tail

bound to this below
land we hold onto
        we lose
flood intrudes

traps miraculous-assed
catfish followed bottom
bit bait absent nests
hush   here's inundation

Search skin

for the faintest hints of light

forming forth

interpolate   another million suns

accompany

the infinitesimal abyss

already adhered

to new domain

shining ultraviolet

cypress

blooms

a face

crash   the sun emerges

cancels on behalf of behaving
we divide what divides us
the über
scant
satchel of disaster
pouring outside your window
holds gurney up
dilated suffering
ample extinct
privacy
practiced origins
with the lack of manners
fuck   put on
a bluray and forget what I didn't say
the night you thought I'd propose
but asked for another high
life
sans axis
warming shadows
scattered over these pupils
air our
liquid emissions
omitted rotund   rotten
solar trellis
sieges a sea of blackholes
surging survival
perpetuates
the time we put time aside

Emaciated stray

turns away
        heeds   *die*

        synchronized

        unsettle

        the young

dream of breeding

bioluminescent

black heights

dual abysses buckle

        yearn for

double degenerate

white dwarfs

The son of death

is the part of me

that learns

nothing

self portrait

I do not ask the wounded person how he feels
I myself become the wounded person

                              —Whitman

a requiem on repeat:
evaporated river puddle
                    no clear career
                    but the wordwand
                                                  I bet we lose
      lay concrete inside me
                    let me be the next decatur street
an office of orifices   the so-bots gleam glorious
                  roasted all the porpoises
                    punished the pages   contagious
                        my body ages   nobody   my editor
    I speak spokes   they axle the exceptional wheel
                            sterling shivers like dirty dishes
                                                  rinsed
                                                  left
                            to chill in the sink

          and   I   baby   left in bath
      momma's never coming back
      said the guillotine to the giraffe
        expanded moments
    and retract   innovated last
persistently reticent vincent
                  administers cinnamon tongues
            gotta spice the devil out   the nostrils
                                      memory's nest
            when I collapse
                  I'll be best   crash courage
                  cast out on the hudson
                  climb down the missip
      classic don't give a fuck
      trills funeral home time
                  I'll type to the death
                  reckless hearse swerves
        into the stars
              gathering loss

Ghosts bathe my insides

lather lament illuminates

extinction outstretched

harmony can't convey

behind firewall

present

fingertips

tapping

void   our tension

from eternity to eternity

we remain

kneeling

jaws of life

I went owl picking
                    this morning
the first one I plucked
            out of the feathered grass
was the last

its intimate petal eyes
                pollenated mask

I could crush him
            fold him
                    into my pocket
to find many years later

this boy on a highway
locked   inside the backseat
of a sheriff's car like a criminal
crying to be let loose
        for his mother
        to also be lifeless
                        in the jaws
        of the serpent
                —life to finish loss
as if it was not needed for survival
                —to finish pain
like it could be consumed
                and digested whole
as if the world could keep going
by feasting on its inhabitants

                Earth holds out
                in its hands
            an abandoned sacrifice
because of a lack of faith
or the ability to protect
                what we create—
                mistakes
We bury them   bury
their mothers
            and bury our bearing
into a soil you can't slither out of
        only plant yourself into

demolished
the snow wake

this morning woke twice
                          each a wider mouth   under bridge
awake   unsure of waking
                          the world quivers in fitted sheets
adjacent room emits:
                          fucking quit it!
like that ill attempt
                          I kinetic   back   I   forth
swinging on a casket
                          between repression's cavities
I have a mind for celebrating loss
                          grenade tucked tight under chest
in a lavender field
                          spiked with bayonets
siblings throw skulls in the snow

Dilated

horrors

deforested

burning

begging

spoon-fed ice

intensive

care unit

injured

aeons

accidents

overwhelm

offspring

prepare 'a

discrete egress

recompense for

the delicacy of doom

assists gerent flesh

nana taught me
to spell *animal*

               after she hoisted me into a dumpster
               later on linoleum combed
my hair with metal yellow kitchen curses
    cut me for using lice excuse to come home
               before school lunch
               her defeated humor preceded her discovery
my memory hoists to save
    when emptied
               constantly fending off ferocity
               an invariable island revering romance
my nana hands me stove pipes   tarnished silver
    me grazing a dead man's playground discarded by family
               directly disposed
my minus humans
        abandoned daily making
        our lost roles
                   return   scold
                   us for missing the *m*—

Absence loses its patience

                   reflection

gores an extinct iris

fears its fire

all pallbearers

collimate error

lessens the equinox

decline

sole prominence

rots   *dead shinin*

applause of the dead

prying blackbirds
void a grave
vacated
nightwalker ascends

     fishnets at the scavi stop
masculine mascara beset
violence inside blush
bracelets wrists rewards
meridian how much you vowed
to disappoint
        oh sweet rage   fig
        of frustration   peeled off pretending
        & poor prodigal
         you will fuck anything
         to never forget
             the *farletta*
             father named you

       osiris' mummy cock
       bandaged between
       your legs   lorn theatre
       net around your thigh
             throat
    everyone's deity
          swallowed sons
  take the train thru
this city & the next
        replenish your death

World supplies

years

      atmosphere after river

                     bottoms

bound to disbelief

bid my nemesis   adieu

underestimated

    guests

           deaths

I am none

        beholden   to

amplitude

I don't calculate loss
                my mother
                        or the date of her birth
                                a scorpio
                october fourth today
                        I know that
                                because   I naked   paid rent
I forgot to call   my friend peyton
                        reminded me   this weekend
                        he still counting
                        deathdays
                two eras   two absences
                since sundials shattered
        a smidgen of great
          experiences exasperated

      how we fill
              empties

                follow orbits
                        cherry blossoms on floorboards
I have all the death I need
                so I stopped counting

Witching mother was often

beyond us

indigenous wilts

apprehends milk   father   son   holy failure

don't know how humanity stands

an absent paradise

the miss takes 8.29.14

brought this on us we bring
to the party the weed the wine
(leave with more booze)
quench our desperate natures
with a seeping lake
of consequence much like murder
stagnant patience
the refusal of this ghost to hold
you too close in aura armpits
my lethal friends
delivered
ultimatum's exception
reaps removal incomplete
mode madness stifle
burning blocks over
grow floodwaters elsewhere
green advantage
runts roughest of all
abscond or
front and center
of st. charles
tracks dug up
empty we
succumb remotely
revive together
listless not anymore
against sure
too poor
see if the quarter
can get you home eventually
evening   am   afternoon
time turned
doubloon despite
its ever presence
my forever taker
we're disturbed
we're distressed
and we dress misbehavior
to escape the site
where our fantasies
lie a little
longer looking
at our levee
horizons
topple

Have I said an increment more than breath

expressed a petrified pitch

you may recognize   as a fellow

soon-to-be-executed prisoner

reaching mortal terminal

together   in a dusty galaxy

                nursing extinction

desperate inflection

you may recognize

your failed prayer's intentions

                fresh ashes to

                throw the river

                what was

                        home

vulning absence

To Megan Burns

what does seeing change of the idea of home

pelican not of marshes
nor oil slicks
before both
a state symbol sewn
vulning

here twelve years
longer than any lived
before I learned
that verb   saw this symbol

to vuln
   long
beaked bloodletting for babies
stuffed stamped and strewn
from beaucoup balconies
beads to bare-blitzed public
parades the plastic image
assumes mother position

those state pride poems
this isn't   one

isn't sun bloodletting to feed us our days?

with what instrument do you wound yourself?

where there was a world   there is now

father

takes his eyes out before bed
cuts apples
raisins them in salads

on my own   I eat apples after
continue the tradition with my children
                              ever I have
time'll make countrytime too
put clementines in our xmas stockings
prepare red sauce from scratch
segment grapefruit   squeeze
them in serrated spoons
the same way we eat our bagels
folded lox   onion   herring
too much cream cheese

sofabed springs twang
used to jump around the den
blaring neil diamond
"coming to america"
you weren't home
empowered ancestors crossing

teachers partial to vulgarities
let me play on the apple IIe
paint in your office
my child digitally fabricates first bike
to scrape knees   feel the first broken bone

there were times I was convinced
you were an enemy
now I reflect
that culprit tolerated me delinquent

you also fought for more time
no family comes without a fight

hitchhiked with us in the snow
midnight man named tony too
picked us up shared
east coast miles
taught me how to fix a flat

all the tiny plastic gobot toys
I enjoyed
long discarded
in favor of
conversation

well after you offered
to put my head through a wall
suppress my own temper
after living with yours

yet may I still be as generous
with my patience

shaving cream
waterpik
and questions

may I always heed
people as you taught me

and may we arrive
identically with full visibility
on earth's impasse

we have no hope
but moments of understanding

you are the core of my name

Come see   blind parents

confuse our names

      gentle lapsing intimacy

in the gradient of reminiscence

flee relic rays

filter inverts the brilliant

as time bulges from black holes

      azaleas evaporate

send someone close   second to none

right back to the mugging hum drum
of living life silent as an order for one
instead of a loud hand molding fantasies
into being maybe that was god's error
the audience of his mission
couldn't forgive him for setting the garden
with a naked awakening
craving for like company
children now too doped up to redeem
humanity may be the most fragile medium
this planet sympathy symphony
in a minor key that the poets sing
been battling the abyss since the beginning
been tattling on our brethren for a pittance
I can't scrape my soul off the bleached coral
I can't escape the mortal
mortar I'm afraid binds nothing
oversaturate the roots and see what grows
compost the roses like brown banana peels
I meant it when I ripped open my shirt
you watched the fault line form
down the middle of my crypt heart
inked with the tears I held in
over the plucked feathers of my family
I still talk to every day
yesterday my father promised me
he would be there to talk until his death
and while I plan to take him up
on such a gracious guarantee
I reminded him that even when he's dead
I will be speaking to him
I'm not sure how he took that
because that's when we both hung up
but that's how I live fully in this world
and fully in the next
until the whole fucking geode crumbles
to gleaming debris
and my graveyard gets folded
into a greater graveyard lapping behind

Rogue against

the filial role

some may refer to

as magnitude

nebulae

slayed creators

forgive

    the need

to get back

    tiny flap of family

    you will see only in—

how many suns

do you need

to tell you this?

absence azaleas
or maxims for my son

Dedicated to Sunday, David, and Clyde Parker

Distractions are directions.

Never let a chance to go.

People in stone houses should blow glass.

Nonsense is my favorite sense.

Never met a line I couldn't cross.

You can't run away from a home you don't have.

Schizophrenia, I consider multitasking.

Devils are the best dance partners.

Toast: *To all the caterpillars…*
                    (unsaid: *that never made butterfly*)

Lose losing.

Our delusions drive us.

Suspect the expected.

Needs are overrated.

The afterlife's too far-fetched to find.

We may be solar typos.

They're all good ideas
                    before somebody else has them.

Write the poems that everyone else breathes.

Never apologize for your existence
        recognizing existence requires multiple apologies.

The opposite of sensational is saliva.

Develop an allergy to allegiance.

Yesterday's a walking graveyard.

Sun's always full.

Absence exceeds presence.

Out of absence grow sun.

The formulae of our ancestors remain

survivor pyres

of shifted polestars

taking up

the second collection

between constellations

pockets empty dusk

erupt spectral fetal

extinction internment

pulsar breakbulk

abates

deported oarsman

hell hoarding money scores
bottlenecked and automated
brake for the piranha land
unfortunate force field of warlords
and jihadi stations maelstroms
refugees hail countries immediately
cordless borders mortared
brick by encrypted brick
spanglish isn't sexy anymore or is it?
plebeians to possibilities and universal disease
the first version of justice still enacted
surveillance for surveillance
prop for prop
hack for hack
absent alms
the future ain't never coming back
a fragmented figment of zero nonsense
the hillbilly beacon of stability
and reverent progress pilfering
primarily by the pilgrims
under whose policies we remain orphans
offspring captured by a decomposing rain
and why should we not damn our withering to spring
and why should we not feel the fluster further
sensitize our oppression and fortunes
to understudies of undertakers
and why should we not care when they don't upstage us
and why should we not fight in the streets for the same fucking thing
everyone fights in the streets for then why should we not exist and exist and
think not of not freely thinking then why should we not believe the sharks and
the remoras are breeding as well as the vultures lions and gazelles and its us
them and the whole fucking periodic table bleeding or drawing blood or fleeing
to attack our prey another livelong eternity which extinction still strikes as the
most bearable and dignified fate even after all the beauty of earth blows into
vacant freezing space like the goodbye kiss it was always meant to erase

Kin

to none   abstain from

prey   into the people

one human mirage

another's divine revelation

fold me   skull-wide

sacrament   inside this poem's mutiny

enforcer exchange   helpless immaculate

we gotta extinct one here

for remote

contrition

absolute

life rattle

          furiously shakin space

bodies clanging earth against atmosphere

    for bambino

      brat with a bowtie

        lessens his toy grip to favor another

      what we want

     buried on the bare living room floor

if god's a scaredy cat

  sun's his night light

who taught him death

       to share   be polite?

      what unknown goon

     did he witness rise?

B/C THAT'S THE STORY I WANNA TELL YOU NOW

the last fable excreted by stellar calligraphy

     illegible constellations between

   extinction:

     when baby Lawd licks the bowl

Can you compact your absence

like I can

    the frontlines of extinction

    we've already infiltrated

    where breath like light

            life's word

traveling the speed

of death

    replete

    day don't save

cold craving

god's apology
        the ransom
a story spoiled
    book you have to die
                to read

the gore preferred
death parasitic
require the river
                    beyond
                survivals which no flesh shall pass

the time   after apocalypse

            alone over an open flame
                of heaven's ashes
                            celestial icarus
                            night nude in
                            sky formaldehyde
                            collapsible   colossus
                                    eclipsed by humanity
                                    thirsts for bonfires of why
                                    awake perpetuates
                                    asking for another
                                    experience to inhale
                                    galaxies re-gifted

Once   divides us

        sheer fallacies

        solar flurries

        detonate words

die my injured elderly

siege shadows

tucked in   eclipse

caused comets to invent

time to absorb

your upcoming

        litany of loss

odes to impermanence

no river if you're sweating
                    or shivering
so much success
      in death
no matter how we redesign dying
no matter how we dress up
                    we drop

*

last weekend
at the ram's horn
sally's not doing good business
trying to sweep the light off the floor

husband's trying to get a good job
being a carpenter or something

*

all that alive are alluvial
rivers dig our own grave

*

she was happy
        to die
                but didn't
when she was pleased
        with life
                goodbye

*

allshedid
allsheneverdid

*

palace packed
patrons not tipping
citizens strolling ghosts
down the street

*

not stray
boulders
nor meteors
planets crash into

shooting stars
die too

*

poems fall like unsupported arches
topple human
supernovas
fail their creator
parapets to invaders

*

the clappers know
we out of ways
of fooling ourselves

indiscreet
DIE
POOF   proof
inside young   precious fetching

what final thoughts do to you

*

remarkable blast cap corrected our orbit
reaching for its share of the heavens

*

still contend death's the final thought
no notice
heard by the next star river azimuth
more   than man
more   than gods
                    division creates
                    symmetry—
                    this existence
                    the only exigence

mortality   darkness

            death is   thirsty

quenched   only   by itself

                    shards to lips
            meaning subsists on impermanence

*

son still holds
the last touch
of his mother's casket
walks around carrying it
like a crush

all this life collecting
evidence death
is tangible

corpses   the rulers
          of Earth

Rising inside

your spectrum

only absence

supplies survival

appendix*

* "Diamonds in Dystopia" is the seed text written for a 2016 TEDxLSU performance debuting an interactive poetry web app that uses a Markov Chain algorithm process to creative datamine a massive amount of text—in this case, over 2500 TED Talk transcripts constituted found texts for improvisation. Project collaborators include digital artist, Derick Ostrenko, and experimental musician, Jesse Allison. We continue to adapt the text corpus database and framework for various event-specific performances, including New Interfaces for Musical Expression (NIME) and South by Southwest (SXSW) as well as interactive fine arts installations.

Diamonds in Dystopia

all know who you are whole-hearted
        you download an episode often
   hold down apostasy jobs
       dancing sunlight in psychoanalysis

     new dimension   new struggle
street view drop in the dow jones
departs on facebook twitter google maps
can't afford allegiance
      rates   the 20th century expressed this
          the positive forces
       eliminate the common denominator
        all regularities
         steps toward unification
      built borderless cheap even free

we farmed fish fisherman
   assign values to the viewer
     when streaming's easy
how we numb
used to watching
      people drown
everybody elements
unraveled connection

each and every year
     wasn't taken for granted
there are 14,000 planes
the amount of salmon   to disappear
   damns EVERYWHERE
but are there interfaces
     that tell of great nature?

we often say to companies
        eating themselves evolve
     it becomes a threat to spark a solution

and we keep growing
attempting to reach outside
        the world and make way
complicit comeback
    of the collaborative
     red-eye flock

don't mind stepping for clean water

the radioactive boys of dust
threaten observers
committed organic

ubiquity of gluttons
outside interference

felt like today

a fish   now two   blooms
mean moon phenomena
symmetries struggle cyborgs

disarm
the certainty of domination
preferred by our elders
coded origins story
defines the nowhered

mode of mud
matter provided
man analyzed Eden
then analyzed

people
the good and grave
one garden   we script war
crosshairs   two tiny lines joined against

our utopia is our apocalypse
cripples water
people shelter
as if concern were an
enforced homelessness
the dream of infrastructure
limited to the global
intimately unscathed
one which does not us
we tool the endless pursuit

manufacturing a hi-tech public
sight-servers

electronics educated
the age of eyes
out of visible energies
arises art
displacing
diamonds in dystopia

                    the conditions that carry
                              fear in the patient
               superb skin
liquid parts light
the shape of your birthday

we want the real and painstaking
               to draw it out as far as planets

everyone who stopped by responded
                                   with a crisis

                                   solution says
                    I would haven
                              withholding petroleum
                              mediated population
                              who doubt today
                    many need its waste

while death builds its answers
I'm gonna compare stars
     go adaptable

25 microbes without
                              we do we knowledge
               come on Earth
                         media
     toxic therapy
                         discuss this expense
               irrigating minds

the one prototype for change
               more giving systems
sea-deep leaks

the justice problem when
I start talking about failure
               won't fix the fissures
               we started for our children

                              joined in diameter
                    drilling their blue stage flame

80% hydrated victorious
        spent to give and give

I dim forever
to touch it for a minute

form

The form of this manuscript derives from a dream I had about reading two books in one, laid out on the left and right side of the page. It also aligns with the paradox contained in the book's title.* The axis poem spans myth, time, and space, and the individual poems function as floating stellar bodies or sun flares orbiting the extended axis poem. Similar to the problems in cartography, 3D bodies get distorted when translated and presented in 2D space, and while I am exploring digital multimedia poetics, the primacy of the page as phenomena combined with the minimalistic beauty of naked print and arduously crafted words reigned for this presentation.

Some poems are sunspots and were written with a methodology I refer to as Event Maps, an observation technique and label borrowed from Hannah Hinchman that I am developing and exploring as I release myself from the rotations and revolutions around the concept of this book. Some of these poems were the gestations of this process and are dictated entirely by concrete events and specific experiences as opposed to the intentions of the poet, which is an opposing yet shared point in space (when figuratively folded) with the abstract poems.

May these lyrics stir your solar wind—

---

* An old line Katie Ford encouraged me to explore as a young writer (I've been toiling over it and its manifestations for decades, and I don't think I'll ever get it perfect in a poem; in fact, the real challenge was editing its omnipresence out of these poems), of which there are several meanings to me related to loss, haunting homelessness, filiation/affiliation, post-Katrina New Orleans, Christian myth, and the paradoxical nature of the universe.

about the poet

Vincent A. Cellucci is the author of *An Easy Place / To Die* (CityLit Press, 2011) and editor of *Fuck Poems* an exceptional anthology (Lavender Ink, 2012). *come back river* (Finishing Line Press, 2014) is a bilingual Bengali-English translation chapbook with the poet and artist Debangana Banerjee. *_A Ship on the Line* (Unlikely Books, 2014), a battleship-collaboration with poet Christopher Shipman, was a finalist for the Eric Hoffer Award. *Diamonds in Dystopia*, an interactive poetry experience, was anthologized in *Best American Experimental Writing 2018*. He teaches communication and digital media in the College of Art & Design at Louisiana State University.

shout outs

First and foremost, to Bill Lavender, friend, mentor, and twice publisher
without whom this book may have never seen the light of day

Eric "Easy" Elliott, my editor

Benjamin Lowenkron for his ear and very influential suggestions on form
and its relationships to heliophysics

Brock, Brooke, & Mina Guthrie; Chris, Sarah, & Finn Shipman; Peyton, Ryan, & Miles Burgess;
Debangana, Suparno, & Irabati Banerjee; and Zack & Jillian Godshall / For being more than
friends and talented poets with great line edits and lengthy conceptual discussions, but
lifetime collaborators
my creative families

Megan Burns, friend, poet, publisher, bad ass, and leader of NOLA poetry family
thanks for giving great attention to this manuscript
and for always calling me out and (not) hooking me up—pesto!

Jonathan Penton and Rosalyn Spencer for their most formidable support,
understanding, and tolerance surpassing their respectable roles in this publishing racket
into generous years of spirited cheers

Dr. Mary McCay for being my bestie, advisor, and mentor with open arms for decades

Dooby for his honesty and brotherhood

Stonefly for sharing the river goddess, captaining the green fish of deserving fools,
and continually giving me the oars to the most beautiful river in the world

Dylan Krieger deserves mention for aiding countless revisions to this manuscript
as she was nearest to my abundant absence and sun longer than anyone

Dean Alkis Tsolakis for enabling this poet
by being the best boss on the planet

Elizabeth Duffy for being the sun
behind the curtains and making my work day-to-day

Professors Derick Ostrenko and Jesse Allison
for sharing their brilliance, collaborating, and traveling with me

To the Moon

Laura Mullen for still being there for me as well as taking the time
to look at an extremely early edition of this manuscript

Ralph Adamo for being a New Orleans poetry seer

Andrei Codrescu for being Andrei Codrescu

Gregg Wilhelm, my first publisher, heretofore and always main man

Chris Tonelli, Matt Rasmussen, Justin Marks, and the entire Birds LLC Krewe
for all the stellar readings, hangs, and hangovers over the years

Luisa Restrepo and Isabel Rountree for getting me to step up my InDesign game

Fos for her generosity with her talents as musician, saw-teacher, stylist, and confidant

Caldonia, my starsniffer

Angeliki for helping me to finalize this manuscript and epoch and float
toward a brighter one

Michael Robinson and "Don Don" Boutte for their glowing roles
aiding and abetting me in attaining a home away from New Orleans

Kris and Gwen Palagi for the dinners, GSM, and their catacombs of attentive listening

Jason and Marsha Vowell for BLARPS, tophats & Madi cu defios x 15(,000 throwdowns)

The Hunts for all the underbelly rubbing of Decatur

Finally, all my running partners all over the planet
but especially friends and colleagues in the NOLA, Lafayette, and BR/LSU
writing and art and design communities—
Thank you

44172361R00068

Made in the USA
Middletown, DE
04 May 2019